The Love/Pain Trials
(*and the Healing)

Money

ISBN: 979-8-9858197-0-0

DEDICATIONS

This book would not be possible if it weren't for everyone I encountered on my journey. Thank you.

The Love/Pain Trials

CONTENTS

The Love/Pain Trials

ACKNOWLEDGMENTS

To my mother:
not everyone can be as blessed to have a parent supporting their art like you. There is nothing in the world I could ever give you to amount to that and that, I will never take for granted. My rock, thank you for holding it down now and forever.

To my family, both chosen and of origin:
this is the first written example of endless years of support, listening, and loving me and what I do. Thank you cannot begin to encapsulate my gratitude for you being in my life to whatever extent that may be – you exist in this book one way or another.
To Lenny in particular, thank you for remembering a random moment when I mentioned I was working on a book, and holding me accountable ever since – it will always mean more to me than you know that you supported this dream simply because you support me.

The Love/Pain

1. THE ORIGIN

I've been surrounded by less friends,
so that means journeys with less ends
and fake people trying to tie up loose ends.

So, excuse me if I lose friends.

2. ODEE

They be telling me I'm Bugging.
They say I'm Odeeing when I finally decide to even speak
of what I should do

           -    but probably won't.

When I finally choose that my boundaries of disrespect
and distaste have been crossed
    and burned
       and played with
          and teetered on the edge with,
now I'M the one that's moving "crazy?"

If you were to see what one could endure behind closed
doors,
    You'd say they're odeeing -
    Or they're bugging -
    Or they're tweaking —
    Or they're wyling -
    Or mutter any usage of Lingo that you could fathom,
    to simply wrap your head around what one would take in
quietly —

for someone else to boast about loudly.

3. HAVE YOU SEEN THAT GIRL?
For Ami circa 2017

Tell me now, have you seen her?

You seem to not understand who I speak of but if
you've ever seen her, you would.

you would understand the light that radiates from her
eyes.
You would understand the unspeakable beauty -

Tell me now, have you at least heard of her?

A live version of exuberance
A being so breath taking-
Gasping for air every time.

Tell me now, have you seen her?

Or have only I been blessed?

A figment of my imagination or of life personified?

4. WHO DAT BOY?

Hol up -
Who that?
Who that?
That's ya bro right?
Ya homie...
I see him but I don't think he noticed me.

Who that?
Who that?
I mean - I guess I'd like to know
What you fucking with baby?
What lingers in your soul?

Who that?
Who that?
That boy got a smile to kill -
a bit of game -
and some words to make my world stand still.

Who dat boy?
Tell me who dat?
tell me what you made of ...
speak to me....
what drives you?
you always known to play tough?
or,
do shawties always fiend for you like wives do?

5. SHAWTY
inspired by "Shawty" by K. Wood$

He think he want me cause I'm bad-
He tryna make me his shawty -

I think he really want me cause I heal feed him.

And one day he'll realize it's like ambrosia —

I think he wants me because I provide a plethora of ailments -

I think he tryna make me his shawty.

Maybe I shed some light on the parts of him he tryna keep in the dark.
I think he wants me simply cause I like him - I show him an affection he knows he missed.

He tryna make me his shawty.

I think he chooses to want me when he thinks he needs me.
I think he wants me when I heal him.

You tryna make me your shawty?

6. NEEDY

I know you want love.
And I know that you need it.

But that shit is not free.
It drains me to give -
so stop hitting me when you're needy.

When you've exhausted all the options in your phone and
doubts in your mind...

Don't hit me when you need me.

7. SINKING

if I sunk to the bottom of the sea,

would you hear me?

if I was just a little less loud,

would you feel me?

if my waist shrunk a few more sizes,

would you see me?

if I was ready to pop pussy at any given moment,

could you heal me?

tell me if I was just a little bit lighter,

would you love this?

if I bite my tongue,

would my silence make you lovesick?

if I was fine enough for your bro's approval,

could you fuck this?

8. TOUNGES

My love speaks in a language foreign to your ears.
You never understood an energy like mine...
A vibration rocking you deep into a core caged by ribs
made of glass -
And a heart built off pride.
And I speak in tongues that you can't look up in a book.

Tell me...
Did you think my Lingo would be around forever?

9. OXYGEN

"I got blood on my knees
Knee deep in guts from the
mud and the trees"

Pitch black nights with a
chilly northern breeze --
a blunt with two fingers
wrapped around it
and a mind filled with
what if's,
and how could I's,
and who am I,
and who are we--

> but I'm choking out
> and I need oxygen please.

I need you to shut your mouth that speaks and open your
eyes that see.

I need you to feel the sensations running through your body-

As if all you are is blind.

10. STATIC

For the sake of the rose,
We must water the thorns.

For the sake of your heaven,
I must excuse your horns.

For the sake of the love
We must play the fool.

For the sake of our sanity -
We think we be tripping,
But we must play it cool.

For the sake of our air,
We can't let the static drown us.

11. WATS WRONG

so, you learned to hum on hymns, and stunt on spends?
Tell me, you learned to bluff ya grin and tough out ya rent?
You learned to love the pain?
Or loved to pretend?

We sit up in corners
Smoke manifesting our lungs
A high creeping behind our eyes...

... the sight of you relaxes me.

so, you learned to run on sins, and front on friends?
tell me, you learned to love ya skin and confront ya end?
you learned to ease the pain?
I mean why pretend?

We sit up in corners
My neck snaps- almost breaking
Eyes bloodshot with rage and smoke...

... the sight of him infuriates me almost as much as it
terrifies me.

12. FIRST F**K

He opened his mouth and spoke words that were like
honey and nectar dripping down…
I felt the sweetness between my thighs

He lay his head and his lips spoke that holy scripture to
me…
as if my body was Ambrosia from the gods- slowly giving
him life.

I thought that first fuck would make you stay—

Shit... I thought you'd love me more after it.

13. CHEVY NIGHTS PT. 1

You got,
Yes you got -
Everything I do want -
For a moment.
For a drive's worth.

Ever since I copped this Chevy
I been feeling so ready
to lend you the keys
and don't worry bout gas -
no you don't gotta pay.

Ever since I copped this Chevy,
I been tryna move steady –
and drive out to see you when I'm finally ready.

14. OVER AND OVER

have you ever seen brown eyes melt into honey skin?
or lips pressed against necks feeding off them like sin?
or fingers that roam
and dig for your treasures?
have you ever felt tongues
that can dig for your pleasures?

have you understood that unspoken passion.....

just breathing and seeking?

15. D.T.B

You ever had somebody say
That they was down for you?
Then turn and lift they noses
like they was looking down at you?
Lying on the spot to save face,
they tryna clown on you.

I never made them feel
like they was stuck with me,
so I feel like they never
kept it a buck with me.
The way they moving now,
That shit might fuck with me.

But now I'm like

--

What the fuck nigga?

--

Bitched out
So it's fuck bitches,
D.T.B
No I don't trust bitches.

16. LITE WEIGHT

Tell me what's your reason for being afraid
Tell me black boy,
why are you a taker?
Tell me black boy,
what makes you so beautiful...
Tell me black boy-
who is your God?

I thought, who is your Christ if his skin glows brown?
Is he 3/5ths a savior?

Are you 3/5ths a man?

Are you what makes me whole?
Are you the very air that gets taken away every time I see
you?

Or are you what hollows me?
Is your voice the very poison that makes me choke?

17. L.O.L
to my lovers who favored fear.

I was "loved out loud"

- In private.

And sometimes

- In front of the homies.

But I wanted to be praised,
not because I felt an entitled need to be claimed,
A title was never my issue.

I wanted us to be understood and move like so -
Sanctioned.

This is us and this is what we do -
But yes. Out loud.

Shouted from the rooftops even
because
we are all worthy of
boastful love
and my boasted love
boosted love to my ego -
Because I felt like I could change fear.

Like I could ignite
passion in peons with no perspective
for
beauty outside of bullshit luxury
that they'll spend their lives to achieve -

… when my luxury was them sitting in my face
doing absolutely nothing. Just being.
I wanted intimacy - out loud.

I wanted the hugs in the street, the random kisses,
the hours laid up, the trips, the trials, the growth,
and the decay —
out loud and all in.

But I couldn't change fear,
no matter how loud I was.

18. COOKIES.
to my lovers who couldn't love me fully.

I remember watching endless situations turned
relationships while mine did what cookies do...
Crumbled.

The irony of it all?
The ones I saw were always from the male perspective,
doused with doubt and sly comments about the women
they were involved with.

Comments like:
"She's type annoying"
"I don't why she's always around me"

And months later I saw happiness emerged from the ashes
of all that locker room talk.

While what seemed to be going well for me did what a
cookie will always do....
Crumble.

19. LOSING SENSE
For JD

I thought I had lost my damn mind
When I had someone sit up in my face after over a year of
occupying time -
And tell me they didn't know if they wanted me.

When I counted the people who loved me and I recalled
words JD had once said to me,

"My first impression of you was powerful. You walked into
the room and it was just YOU"—
I knew I had lost my damn mind and my damn sense when
I let romantic partners treat me otherwise.

I had to realize that my platonic loves know no fear, no
toxicity, no shame.

But my romantic ones… that was another story altogether.

20. WHAT IS LOVE?

how many of us done
gave up our heart for a piece of that art,
you know a piece of that love,
a lil validation and a hug,
a body to hold and that feeling of luck,
a lil *mwah-mwah* and a body to fuck --
somebody to listen to the emotions that you shove,
yo how many of y'all thought y'all been in love?

          they don't tell you in the guidelines that -
              love is powerful and love is pain,
               love is selfish and love is vain,
          love shows itself in the sickest of ways,
        and love shows itself on your darkest of days.

love...
           love lives in the heart of your homies.
when some days they were the only ones who could hold
me
so, when we're breaking down over love that we "knew,"
you see who's really there and who really loves you.

         Cause love shows itself in its moments of lack-
           where you're constantly picking up slack,
            because it shows you what your limits are.

What you're willing to do
and what would leave some scars.

              love finds its way to hurt you
              while also forcing you to grow.

love is desire and sometimes hate.
love is blatant and love is straight
love ain't always "straight" but it's straight up —

it's under your skin and up in your face
because without that love…
you feel like you wouldn't have no place.

Tell me,
where is the love for yourself?
Like grabbing more off that shelf,
and force feeding that shit down your throat,
like you was coarse bleeding for growth --
you forced that love to your dome
where is the love in your home?
so, how many of us done "been in love" just to have
somebody to phone?

No one tells you how easy it is to fall in love and how hard
is it to stay there.

Cause love might play nice but love don't play fair,
and when I scrambled for love she let me lay there,
loving on maybe's and red flags like a fucking state fair.

And when love told me to wait I asked him "wait where?"
he said stick around and maybe one day, my love might
play fair.

So, I gave love some years till I set love free.
But we're simple creatures sometimes, so we love what we
see.
You see I always loved love…
but did love ever love me?

The Healing

21. SOMEONE'S SOMETHING

Here's to being both eye candy and soul food.
To being more than someone's
Daughter,
Wife,
Sister,
Friend.

Here's to being the you they stifled for so long.

22. ODE 2 U
For Sabrina

My soulmate always said that if she could, she'd write
"an ode to my hands."

I never knew if that honor came from my writing ability or
for the simple fact that my hands rolled us flowers and
herbs in our best and worst moments.

I never told my soulmate that if I could, I'd write
an ode to her soul.

That honor comes from being one of the only people in
this life to see me clearly.
A true reflection of me.
Our relationship existing as a constant reminder to water
that which waters me.

23. PRAYERS

I don't see the problem when you tell me that you just
doing you,
But maybe the truth is that the worlds screwing you
So,
when you look at you tell me, can you stomach that view?

Well... can you?

I hope you haven't reached the point where you're praying
to shed your skin in hope that it sheds some sins

and I pray that you been hoping to find your solace in
something other than artificial faces that make loving
yourself seem so basic.

I don't see the problem when you tell me that
you just doing you…
But maybe the truth is that
the worlds screwing you.

Maybe hating the world
made you love yourself.

I hope the prayers I've said for you in silence
have been whispered into your ear.

24. A LIGHT IN THE ADDICT

I been feeling like all I got is time -
Time it correctly.

my mind has been on auto pilot.
working at its own will.
not sticking to one moment
or reminiscing on a short term emotion.

I've been writing words -
to later forget why they're there.
I've been feeling so strongly -
to later forget why I cared.

I been feeling like I'm running out of time -
Timer going off - and I forget why I'm here

25. SINCE WAY BACK

I remember way way back,
When I used to look at you like that..
Praying one day that you would look back,
And figure if you even wanted me like that....

And you said that you think about me every day,
Something like Saturday to Saturday...
Saying I'm on your mind for 7 days...

So for so long,
I've been caught in the middle of the
boxing match in my head…
Ali and Frazier…
taking every jab and uppercut to the face trying to ask
myself…

What are you on?
You gotta let me know something...
What are you on?
gotta let me know one thing....
What are you on?
Tell me was my mind right when it kept screaming that you
were bad news like ...

26. TIME SPENT

I spent so much of my life fearing the feeling of weakness
Or maybe the appearance of it -

Because what a shame it would be to go through everything
I do and not come out of it stronger, or at least appearing
as such.

I spent so much of my life understanding my sensitivity as
weakness.
So I feared my emotions for as long as I could remember
their formations.

27. MIRRORED
For Omari

When I lost all faith in the men that surrounded me,
        you returned like a phoenix from the ashes.

I had been so sure that placing trust in men who have time
and time again hurt, abandoned, and abused me was my
downfall –
        that I was to blame for people's misuse of me.

Then you showed me a love I forgot I knew.

You showed me self-doubt, introspection, a love for life,
fear, and praise… all by showing me yourself.

And in turn…
        you showed me myself.

I needed to accept how different we were to also
understand, we have always reflected both the best and
worst parts of one another.

And I'd have it no other way.

28. LOW DOWN DIRTY BLUES

"That be me, love unconditionally "
Innocently stripping the Nineteen years of what I thought
love was.

That be me, living so freely
fighting to see it clearly
trying to higher my pitch or tone
so that you can see me sweetly --

That be me digging deep
all for my dignity
trying to lift my energy
finding divinity in me.

That be me tryna perfect my time
so that it's worth it.

29. INJUSTICE

The biggest injustice I've done to myself was not trusting my intuition....

That gut feeling and third eye vision that my mother gave to me, and our ancestors gave to her.

The biggest injustice I've done to myself was subjecting myself to the same patterns, with the same people, to see if they'd change.
Like poking the same bear won't make it mad...

I did myself a disservice and carried out my biggest injustices to myself whenever I allowed external thoughts, opinions and situations change how I feel and see myself.

When I allowed things that degree of control, I had officially lost.

30. APOLOGIZE

I seek closure in people who couldn't care less to provide
it.
I blind myself with the image of you that I want so badly.

But I don't want you....
I want your positive qualities.

I bind myself with my own empathy till I'm bleeding out.
And it's okay to feel sorry sometimes.

I curse myself with nights of suffering all because I want
that image of you.
I hate that you made me feel sorry sometimes.

But I don't want you.
I only wanted you to care.

31. INNER CHILD

She's gripping at my leg -
Clawing at it even.

I can't help but feel like I'm dragging her with me.

Dragging her trauma,
And her pain,
And her fear of abandonment
And her fear of being misunderstood
And her fear of being too big and too much for the spaces
she's in, the places she goes and the people she's with.

I'm tired of feeling like I'm dragging her like dead weight.

All I want is for him to get up and hold my hand,
                                        just walk with me.

32. PEER PRESSURE

I roll up so much cause
My flowers never hurt me like you do.

You feel pressured —
to puff pass it down
2 the next chick,
exhaling all your
insecurities
so she could
b the next hit.

I inhale some words
Exhale some distress

I inhale my intuition till I'm seeing in code.
Exhale some lost thoughts till I'm
losing my soul –

But that's where I got it twisted.

In letting myself think that you could take me away from
what I know of who I am…

is where I let you get me fucked up.

33. C.T.A.C

"It's been a minute since we last kicked it"

It's been a while since I've seen my energy thrive, since I've
seen God...

It's been a minute since I've looked between the lines.
Through every crack and crevice that forms me.

If you could pick up the phone and tell me it was real,
I can show you my process and everything it took for me
to heal…

If I could be scarred by every
"what if" that was fed to me -

if only I could be left in a casket
full of marks,
and kisses and bruises
from the pain inflicted on my vulnerability -
Maybe then you'll see me as the masterpiece I carry myself
as.

34. CRAVINGS

For years I craved a lover who would ask me what my
needs are
... who would just simply ask me how I wanted to be loved
and cared for.

Until I got it.

Then I quickly realized...
I did not want to spend my hours and my days drawing up
a blueprint,
Laying out a rule book for my lovers on how to deceive
me.

I wanted a love to consume me and at the same time make
me feel whole,
I wanted a love to show me myself in my entirety....
while allowing me to show them theirs.

I did not want a lover to ask me so that they could change
their ways.
I wanted a lover so fully themselves that I felt loved and
cared for exactly how I needed.

35. CHEVY NIGHTS PT.2

I seek closure in people who couldn't care less to provide it.
I blind myself with the image of you that I want so badly.

But I don't want you....
I want your positive qualities.

I bind myself with my own empathy till I'm bleeding out.
And it's okay to feel sorry sometimes.

I curse myself with nights of suffering all because I want that image of you.
I hate that you made me feel sorry sometimes.

But I don't want you.
I only wanted you to care.

36. REFLECTION/FEAR.

Why God, why God do we gotta fear?

I never knew fear until I did not know who was staring
back at me.
Until I realized that the woman I once thought I knew I
was -
has transformed.

She's looking back at me now with lost eyes and a confused
grin.
She looks like the mix of tequila and sprite.
Dangerous yet Sweet.

Life's a bitch, pull her comfort to the side now.

"I'm here to remind you that you don't know yourself like
you claim to."

She looks back at me with an ulterior motive.
She looks like a mix of Heaven and Hell.
Holy yet Damned.

I grew accustomed to more fear.
I grew comfortable with her grin.

I had never known fear until I met the one who has staring
back at me.

Why God, why God do we gotta suffer?

37. WHERE WE HAIL FROM

"If you are silent about your pain, they will kill you and say
you enjoyed it."
- Zora Neale Hurston

Do you know where you're from?
I know I'm Brooklyn born. 212, 718, 347, 646 represent
Or do you hail from the west side?
Maybe your family is from chi town by way of the dirty
south.
Do you know where you're from?
Label yourself as lost and misguided
And I don't blame you
Misplaced and taught that -
we were pieces of property waiting to be owned,
land waiting to be colonized,
crops and fresh soil waiting to be cultivated.
Do you know where you are from?
As far as they're concerned
breaking you down is just a means to an end.
It's just lovers to friends,
it's just Takeover to Ether,
It's just that neither can we hurt.
We are the children of misfortune.
Children of the problems and forsaken.
We are the flowers blooming from dead soil.
Much like roses that grew from concrete,
our souls too strong to stay grounded.
Our roots feed life like ambrosia to the gods.
We are as light as the holy spirit and as dark as darkness
itself.

38. LETTERS TO THE ROSTER PT.1

It's not crazy that I loved you…
it's crazy that I looked at you and saw potential --
rather than the simple, vision lacking individual that you are
-
that shit is crazy to me.

I wish you could shut your mouth long enough so that your
eyes could see but
you just blind your eyes so that your mouth could speak
and
you never really listen,
you just be waiting to talk.

I really hate that you're stagnant.
I wish you wanted to find your purpose as much as I
believed you had one.

You see, I wished you could see me clearly
But your waters run shallow so how could you ever see me
deeply?

you're simple … AS FUCK
- yet I miss you.
but you don't really stimulate my mental,
your bullshit is now predictable,
and every red flag is no longer invisible,
it's despicable really.

I know you'd rather have a good time than a good thing —

every boy wanna be a man but stay the same,
     just scared reflections but with longer limbs and a fade
          - they never really change.

and he's complacent.
               so, I got tired of "complaining."

I wish he believed his dreams as much as I'm willing to
          chase them
     but I can't change him.
     and trust me I never wanted to.

I hope when he looks in that mirror, he can stomach that
          view,

it's not crazy that I loved -
          but it's a little crazy that I loved you.

39. SCAR/SCARE

I had to learn to move with love daily -

While still operating with the understanding that in the
span of a year,
a month,
a week,
a day & a night,
someone could just wake up
and not fuck with you anymore-

They may say otherwise but you feel the energy shift,
you notice the actions change -

Everything becomes very…
Touch and go.
Hot and cold.

The thought scars me more than it scares me.

40. LETTERS TO THE ROSTER PT.2

In your absence I had to learn how not to hate you.
I had to learn that it was never about me,
because I was patient -
but even the most patient get tired of waiting
so, I put some distance.
And you showed me you lacked persistence.

it's funny that I had your people sitting in my face
like he never had a chick like you that's taking up this space
and I swear I been a cynic -
or maybe it's acidic,
putting poison in my head like it's not you,
I was to blame.

Cause I knew the game I played,
and I knew the wicked ways
that everything could twist and turn,
but I'm stubborn,
had to learn.
I had to see it through,
to find out what I always knew,
it's never me because it was always you.

Looking back on it,
I knew that shit was a mess
you was out here holding cards while I was out there
playing chess.

This shit was never about me.
I was always a projected view
of how you felt about you --

So, it's not crazy that I loved,

                    but it's a little crazy that I loved you.

ABOUT THE AUTHOR

Money, A.K.A ATMoney, A.K.A ATM is a Queens & Brooklyn born and raised multi-media hyphenate. With their first talent and passion being poetry, Money has always been dedicated to arts of expression. Money is simply put, a student. A student of the system, student of the game, student of life, a student of their people and of their ancestors. So much power in one *small* word (student) that's been stripped and taken away yet, we fail to understand that just because we are students does not mean we are not educators and teachers and nurturers of the minds, bodies, and souls around us.